Love Help
and Serve All

Sarbjit Basra

Love Help and Serve All

ISBN: 978-0-9569660-0-1

Published by Sarbjit Basra

This edition was published in 2011

Printed by Anchorprint Group Ltd

**"My humble salutations to the
Great Divine Universe"**

Our life is a book

Each day is a page

Every event is a chapter

This book Love, Help and Serve All is like a lotus flower. As we read the words, the sentences will go inside our consciousness and start to unfold petal by petal; bringing so much love, bliss and positivity into our bodies that these blossoming attributes will begin to reflect into our lives. As you read page by page, yourself and others will start to notice the changes in attitudes and behaviour. Day by day we will begin to experience:

Loving thought is truth

Loving action is righteousness

Loving feeling is peace

Loving understanding is non-violence

The end of education is character

The end of wisdom is freedom

The end of culture is perfection

The end of knowledge is love

Where there is faith, there is love

Where there is love, there is peace

Where there is peace, there is truth

Where there is truth, there is bliss

Where there is bliss, there is God

Life is a game, play it

Life is a challenge, meet it

Life is a dream, realise it

Life is love, experience it

Love gives, by giving and forgiving

Self-lives by getting and forgetting

There is only one religion, the religion of love

There is only one caste, the caste of humanity

There is only one language, the language of the heart

There is only one God, he is Omni-present

Once you have read this book, you will feel like a newly reformed human being radiating so much love and light into the lives of others around you. Problems, troubles and illnesses will become a thing of the past, as all these things were only created by us with our minds. Only after you have finished reading this book will you realise WHO and WHAT you really are. Before that you were three people:

The one you thought you were; the one others thought you were; now you are the one you really are.

From this day on you will never need to change your personality. Congratulations! You have found your real inner self and not what others wanted you to be.

This book is dedicated to each and every one of you either holding or reading it at this very moment; it is dedicated to our beloved Mother Earth and the Divine Universe. You are reading this book not by chance but by the divine order of this Universe because your soul has already reached a level where it is now ready to move on to the next dimension of understanding and enlightenment. If you read this book very carefully, paying close attention to what concepts and meanings stand out to you and you try to take it in then you will truly gain the wisdom and light aimed to reach out and touch your soul. All these words that are written will manifest and become the essential food for your thoughts. I wish to thank you for taking your most valuable and precious time to read this and I pray with all my heart that between us we can and will gradually make all the little changes equating to the overall mass change to the planet. Doing so will mean that we can eventually create and live in a place where love, peace, consideration, caring and sharing, giving and forgiving and all other divine virtues and principles begin to start cultivating within all of us. These divine virtues will also cultivate in our beautiful and wonderful Mother Earth, the universal womb that we have been so divinely blessed and fortunate to be living in. I care deeply about each and every one of you, Mother Earth and all the animals and creatures that it loves, nurtures and inhabits. I would be greatly privileged with the grace of the divine Lord to answer any questions arising from this book to the best of my insight and ability. I hope and pray Mother Earth and the Great Divine Universe will continually guide me with the answers and blessed knowledge to help fulfil my service, as service to man is service to God (The Great Universe).

Lovehelpandserveall@mail.com

www.lovehelpandserveall.com

There are numerous books that are available which have been written by so many different people, but this particular book you are holding this very moment is flowing nectar of words that have poured out from deep inside my heart. Consider for a moment that the heart itself is such a unique and magnificent organ. It has a multitude of different abilities. We only have one heart however that one heart has the ability to not only makes us laugh but make us cry, not only make us love but to also make us care and all the other emotions that it's able to encompass. Think to yourself how many other organs in the body are you aware of that can operate in such a complex but beautiful way as does the heart.

Chapter One

Consider for a moment the analogy that our whole life itself is like a book, each day is a page and every incident is a chapter. When we go to sleep we all have different dreams, some we remember and some we forget. Now whilst dreaming we meet a whole spectrum of so many different people, some still living amongst us, some whom have already passed over and some we may not even recognise. Our dreams seem so real at the time, however it is only when we awake that we realise we were merely dreaming. We may have so many wealthy possessions and important roles in these figments of deep consciousness and sleep but soon as we open our eyes and find ourselves lying wherever we may have fallen asleep, and only THEN do we come to realise that we could not bring back with us the dream, the people or things left behind in that surreal dreaming state. Instead everything in our dreams is left behind even the body we are in, as our own body has always remained wherever our soul has left it asleep. All these experiences of dreaming are living proof to us that this life of ours is no different to the dreams, or its superficial and material components. One day we are going to wake up yet again somewhere else where our soul has left us asleep and this life of ours and everything contained within it is no more real than a dream as everything else, possession or treasures will remain here again left behind. The only thing that we will be able to leave and take with us is our soul and the inner virtuous treasures and noble deeds you have accumulated over many lifetimes. I plead with you to take a look at your own dreams so that you realise that nothing or no one is going to go with us when we leave. That is why we should not take anything or anyone for granted as there will come a day when we are going to leave all loved ones, near and dear, all wealth and possessions behind us. This then leads us to the question that once we know what the truth is then why can we not be kind and considerate towards everyone and start to make changes within ourselves and our way of thinking and our behaviour? Please let's make this a better and friendly place to live in.

All that most of us wish to do is to live an acquired peaceful life and be there for one another. After all what is man alone? As only when there is more than one does it become a unity, a community. We need each other to make our beautiful moments so enjoyable and memorable. If we were to lock ourselves all alone away from the rest of the world, what can we possibly achieve from doing so? We would only find ourselves imprisoned within and yet the sad thing is that most of us still continue to live in this imprisonment whilst living amongst our brothers and sisters. Not knowing your true self is almost as if you are a prisoner in your own body.

If only we could retreat by withdrawing from our outer self, and take a step inwards to our inner self. This is the only time when truly we can begin to recognise the real person within. Every time we look outwards from the eyes of our soul we begin to merge what we see outside of ourselves based on what is happening around us, especially when it comes to our ceiling on desires, our tastes and senses. It is almost like taking a peep out of a dark hole sitting in a dark room, having no idea of what else is in the room with you due to the darkness.

As soon as we make that hole and look out then we can easily start and become a part of the world we start to see. It is like the times when we are watching a movie. How often do we forget where we are and what we are watching? We get so engrossed with the movie that we become a part of it. It is only when the movie comes to an end that we realise that we were only watching it and were never a part of it.

The same thing happens with our everyday living. Our outer world makes us become something different to our real inner personalities. This is why we should and need to listen to our inner voice, which is the real us, not our voices or our minds but our consciousness (Atma) which is the real us.

Our mind can make us become fifty different people in one day, and from the fifty people how do we know which one is the real true self? We have no idea until we develop the ability to be still and quiet and to go inside of ourselves and listen to the inner voice. There are some people who may call this meditation, others may call it communicating with our higher self. Always remember that we are three people. The one we think we are, the one others think we are, and the one we really are.

It is very important for us to identify ourselves, we can live our whole life and never know who we really are because circumstances and the people around make us become who and what they wish us to be. Like robots or puppets we have become just that. Take for example in your early years of soul development, your parents made you become the way they chose to bring you up, then you meet friends who want to turn you in to something else resulting in a confusing conflict within your mind. This conflict is further fuelled by our partners who also try to turn us into something they wish us to be. This leads to the fundamental question..... Who are we? Or better still, what are we? We have no idea of who and what we really are, because all we have done is become different personalities for the different people in our lives. We do this just so that we can be accepted by our loved ones and the society that we live in.

There is a saying, "you can't please other people, but thank God you can please yourself".

We need to realise that we are different individuals. We have come into this world all alone and we will leave this world all alone. There is not one person or not one thing that will go with us, so what are we really taking with us? What have we really achieved? All our lives we have cheated and lied in order to fit into the society we live in just so that we are accepted by the people around us. We have tried to please our parents, families, friends and colleagues. Guess what…Were we really able to please any of them? Well no, because they themselves don't know what they are or who they are either. So by running here and there, bending backwards for them was never going to score us any brownie points.

Instead of us confusing our minds by trying so very hard to become what others want us to be so that they will accept us, we should in fact know exactly who and what we really are. Then let others accept us for that very reason. If there is someone who doesn't want to accept you then it is in your own interest to walk away from these kind of people. Once we know who and what we really are then throughout the rest of our lives there should be no change in our personalities. We need to be in control of our senses and mind. Instead we let our monkey mind control us.

There are many moments when we want to do one thing and suddenly our conscience will make us do another. Our conscience will make us realise that what we were thinking, was not the right thing for us, and it will always stop us from doing wrong. Whether we like it or not, whether we want to or not, our conscience will always take the lead. We will have no choice but to follow. If we don't have our conscience there to guide us then we are no more than walking zombies. For conscience is the most important part of us. It is only then we can actually call ourselves human beings.

The Great Divine Universe has blessed us by giving us just that. It gives us strength and courage to be able to live an honest life, being true to ourselves and to others around us. When we lie, cheat and steal we are not deceiving others any more than we are deceiving ourselves. This is because we didn't have to shut our conscience out of our lives when making that decision to be unfaithful to ourselves and others. How many times do we encourage our children, family and friends to lie on our behalf? Yet, at times we tell our children and families how wrong it is to tell lies. It takes us a whole lifetime to build our trust between all our loved ones and yet one little lie can demolish relationships along with our faith and trust, so before we think of ever telling even a little white lie let us work out what we are about to lose in exchange for that deception as one lie will always lead to another lie. If you lie once you may lie a hundred times.

Again and again we need to be honest no matter what. What sort of an example are we setting for our family and friends or anyone who is a part of our lives? If only we can be honest and truthful our own reflection in behaviour will make them realise what sort of foundations we are laying for them to follow. The saying "thou shall not lie", do we really take notice of this phrase? We may have grown up, and our bodies may have changed but how much we have grown up in our spirituality actually shows a recognisable change in our attitude and behaviour? There is nothing in life that is impossible, as everything is very much possible. There is nothing that we cannot do, if we put our hearts and mind to it.

How often do we stop and take a good look at ourselves and realise just how much capability we have to achieve almost anything? Yes anything and yet some of us have allowed other people to take away our confidence and our courage. We spend all our lives seeing ourselves through other people's eyes. We really need to stand in front of a mirror and take a look at ourselves from our own judgement and not from the opinions of others. Go ahead and look at yourself in the mirror and say "Hello, do you know from this moment on both you and I are going to become one? First, we need to get to know one another, I will start off by listening to you, instead of telling you what to do, how and when." It is going to be like going on a date but, with yourself, so that your inner self gets to know your outer self. You can for once become whole.

All organs, body, mind, thought and senses need to be one. Our mind tells us one thing and our thoughts and brain tells us another thing. Do we know how separated we have become from ourselves? We become to feel that we are living with a total stranger. Our real personality has been trying to reach out to our inner self and all we have done is push it to one side and pretend it's not there as we are so busy trying to please others.

Chapter Two

We are born on different paths with different fates and destinies. We should be telling ourselves to help, to live our lives in the way that we are meant to be living it and not in the way that we would like to. Time waits for no one as every second is precious and is ticking away. The moment we are born, we are placed in a queue of death. The only difference from our family and friends is that nobody knows what order we are all placed in. We don't know whose number is going to be up before whose. We need to live our lives to the full. We need to thank the Great Divine Universe for giving us such beautiful rental bodies as our health is our wealth. It is called a rental body as it is only loaned to us for the period of time we are on this earth, and when our agreement comes to an end our body is left here and the soul leaves. But one important thing to remember is that the soul never dies.

Our body is like a car. A car is only able to function with an engine in it as our body is only able to manoeuvre about when the soul is contained in it. Without a soul, our body is just a corpse as a car without an engine is just a shell. We are never satisfied with our body, we don't like this and that about it. We put on a few pounds and we begin to think it's the end of the world. We spend most of our lifetime focusing so much on the outside of our body frame that we forget to enjoy and appreciate our beautiful bodies for the way they are. We need to thank our bodies for putting up with so much of our nonsense. We get so carried away always trying to compare ourselves with someone or other that we forget that life is made for living and not competing. There was a gentleman walking along the road who was moaning at the Great Divine Universe feeling so sorry for himself because he did not have a pair of shoes, he moaned and moaned until he came across another person who had no feet. There is always someone less fortunate than us.

Instead of spending so much time and money on rectifying this and that about our bodies we should always remember that our true wealth is our health. Let's stop ourselves from punishing our beautiful bodies and fall in love with ourselves for what we are. Only then will others start to love us. If we keep on criticising ourselves then how can we ever expect others to love us for what we are? Two people can never be alike. So, why should we be comparing ourselves to anyone else? There is some difference even in a set of twins, whether it is in their personality or their looks.

Real happiness and contentment is a treasure that lies within each and every one of us. No matter how hard we try we can never find happiness or contentment anywhere outside of our bodies, which is our real inner self. Once we are able to find that inner contentment then everything around us becomes our happiness. We could be living in a big mansion with servants, but if we don't have that inner contentment and happiness then those things will not mean anything to us. The materialistic things in our lives can only put a smile on our faces for a few moments, but the real happiness that is within ourselves can never stop us from smiling.

That is why time is so very precious; every second that we are living should not be wasted. We should at all times be in total bliss and appreciate all that we have. We should be doing this instead of focusing on the things that we don't have which we may never need in the first place.

We get so engrossed into ourselves, which turns to misery which is created by ourselves. A simple smile that costs nothing can stop us from being so miserable. Then what can we teach our children? Are we not meant to be the role models for them to follow? Before we know it our life will have flashed by and the time has come for us to depart. What are we going to take with us? Exactly, nothing! There is nothing that can go with us, not money, cars, house, family, friends or even the clothes that we are wearing. There was a king who was about to die. A little boy approached the king and kindly asked the king if he could take a gift for his grandfather who had already passed over. The king agreed to take his gift with him and would give it to his grandfather when he saw his grandfather after his passing over to the other side. The next day the little boy gave the king a needle and said "this is my gift to my grandfather." All through the night the king could not work out how he was going to be able to take that needle with him to give. He realised for the very first time that he may be a king and have all the riches and wealth, but he could not see how he could take anything with him from his wealth to a little needle. There he was as a king ruling the people of his kingdom and yet it took a very small child to show him that his wealth, family or his servants would not be able to go with him.

We need to remind ourselves that we came into this world with nothing and we are going to leave this world with nothing and no one. It is very important to be happy and blissful and to enjoy every moment that we have as the next moment may never arrive. So, why should we not help one another and be there for others at a time of need. Let's help others unconditionally, because we were fortunate to be in a position to be able to help them in the first place.

It is important to remember we can stop money from overruling our minds and thoughts. Money was made by man and it was made for spending, so that we can buy things but these are things that belong to no one, as we are all going to leave everything behind one day. Money is a very bad thing if we let it overrule our heads, thoughts and mind. Can money buy us peace, health or happiness, if we keep it saved all the time? Can money buy us time? No amount of money in the world can buy anyone time, so how much money do we realistically need? Yes, we need money to pay our bills and put food on the table, but do we necessarily need millions of pounds? Yes, it is good to have money and there is nothing wrong with having it. How much money do we need to spend on ourselves, or are we not human enough to help others? If we are in a position to help those who are in desperate need of our money, a few pence or a few pounds surely that will not make a big loss to our pockets.

We may not be in a position to help the whole world but we can make a start somewhere. What is the point in us having so many properties, houses or possessions? We may even only spend a few weeks of the year being in them. What's the point if we cannot be bothered to put our hands into our pockets and help build free hospitals with free health care for the less fortunate ones or build free schools for those who can't afford to pay for their education? Why are we not able to do all the little things so they would be able to make something of their lives, enabling them to learn how to read and write, as the final fruit of education is character! These small but thoughtful ideas full of energy and healing could collectively manifest into a reality and if we really want we could build small shacks where free food would be distributed for those who for some reason or another are less fortunate than ourselves.

If we were all born with a pen and paper with the ability to write our own destiny and fate wouldn't we all be in a better position? As it so happens, we are all living in the Kaliyuga (dark era) a time where we are required to stick together amidst the chaos, pain and all the natural disasters. We need to hold hands in unity as one fighting against the injustice that we face today. We need to help one another, as there are so many people who are suffering all around the world through no fault of their own. In the world that we are living in, some people are so busy chasing after money, oil, power, name and fame. Yet, deep in everyone's heart we should all know that just like a click of a finger our time is going to come when our soul, without saying a word, is going to leave our body and this world behind.

Each and every one of us is going to have to leave. I don't know of anyone who has been fortunate enough to have lived in this world forever. Millions of humans came before us and went and millions will continue to come and go after us. We need to stop chasing after power, name and fame and start using that time to help one another. Is it really going to break us if we lend a helping hand? We can all try and make changes to stop fighting and tearing each other apart. Look at what we are doing to Mother Earth! Instead of praying to Mother Earth and thanking her we are spilling so much cold blood on her and destroying her. Day by day we are becoming murderers towards Mother Earth. We have destroyed and polluted the rivers and seas as we have no respect for the world that we are living in.

Only after the last tree has been cut down,

Only when the last river has been polluted

Only after the last fish has been caught

Only then man will realise that man cannot live alone on money

(Ancient Native American saying)

How can we call ourselves human beings with the way that we are acting and behaving? We are worse than animals as they can be excused for their behaviour. We as human beings are supposed to have had an education and common sense. We need to stop fighting, and ask ourselves what exactly is it that we are fighting for? For each and every one of us is living on borrowed time and borrowed bodies. There is nothing in this world that we own and there is nothing that belongs to us. Not our possessions, family, friends or our children. The honest reality and truth is that we own nothing and the sooner we accept that the quicker we can stop destroying one another and replace resentment with love. Bring caring and sharing back into our lives.

Let's make this world a better place, let's start to thank Mother Earth, let's love all our brothers and sisters, let's hold hands and join forces, let's help one another as we need to change this world. If we don't then there will come a day when through our hatred for each other there will be nobody left to survive. What will happen to power, oil, name and fame? Believe me, if we don't change our habits, thoughts and behaviour then the day will arrive when there will be nobody left on this earth. If and when that day finally does arrives what has anyone of us achieved from doing all this?

Is this why we choose our politicians, to teach us things like these? Is this what we want our children to learn as they are growing up? No, we want our children to learn how to live in peace and harmony. They need to develop love for themselves, the nature, the world and the rest of the people in their lives. They need to learn how to respect their elders, only then can love help them to survive throughout these natural disasters. We need to remove the word hate from our lives and replace it with love, care and share. Also, learn to practice love, care and share.

Let's change ourselves so that the rest of the world can change itself. There are twenty-four hours in the day. Let's take a few minutes out of each week to lend a helping hand or to sit and send out good thoughts for the peace and welfare of our world. Let's put our hands in our pockets and take out a few pennies, as those few pence may not make any difference to us but will make a whole new change to someone else's life. We can make changes as it still is not too late, otherwise if we don't do it now then there will come a day when it will be too late and we won't be given another chance to put it right.

Everything will be lost and it will be down to each and every one of us, because we were so wrapped up in ourselves. Our thoughts, wants and desires that have caused us to forget consideration and thoughts for others. Our thoughts become actions, let's learn to love ourselves then love the next person to us. Let's learn to love our bodies and thank our bodies with all of our might. We should show gratitude towards ourselves, loved ones and to Mother Earth. The word 'love' is only a four-letter word, but the meaning is very powerful.

Chapter Three

One way of achieving the peace and serenity in your hearts and minds which will eventually cause you to create these positive and pure actions is through meditation. Meditation is so very simple and easy that even a small child is able to meditate. We don't need to be sitting in one place with our legs crossed. We can meditate whilst walking or even doing our everyday chores. Our body can carry on functioning as it usually does, meditation is done with our minds. Yes, I admit at the beginning it is easier to be able to sit still as we don't know what to expect. It could be like a child when they take their first steps. Let's try and meditate. There are so many different ways we can do this. Some people may do it sitting on the floor with their spine straight and their legs crossed. Some people may meditate sitting on a chair, others meditate listening to their breathing whilst taking each breath. Breathing in and holding their breath for a few seconds, and then breathing out.

We can, if we want, hold our thumb touching our index finger so as to make a circle, or place our hands on our lap with our palms facing up. The most important thing is that we have to realise for ourselves what position feels comfortable for us. Until we feel we are comfortable only then will we be able to proceed to the next stage. You may have to find so many different positions before you begin to feel relaxed and comfortable. Although we are always in charge and in control of ourselves, we just forget this with our busy hectic lifestyles. Some people tend to put a light around their bodies for protection. Now we need to close our eyes, don't force your eyelids to stay closed together. Slowly, gently close your eyelids and take a deep breath.

It will take a few moments for us to feel relaxed. Only the slow deep breaths will start to make us feel at ease and comfortable. Some people may even fall asleep but that's fine, everything takes time to learn. Remember the saying, "Rome wasn't built in a day". It will take a different period of time for each and every one of us. So, that is all we have to do is to gently and slowly close our eyes, take slow deep breaths. There will be so many different scenes appearing in our thoughts.

Soon as we realise our mind is beginning to drift we need to keep bringing our mind back and try harder, slowly and calmly empty our minds. Remember we have got a monkey mind that never stops jumping, but this is the first step in trying to control our minds. It is not going to be easy as everything in life needs effort, although it is going to take some work. Slowly we will begin to enjoy that meditation because it will make us feel so relaxed like we have never felt before. So, keep on gently fighting with your mind by trying to push any thoughts out of the way. Remember, if the mind is doing its job to the full by trying to distract us then we also should be doing our duty to the full by pushing the thoughts that arrive out of sight and out of mind.

Slowly it will begin to get easier, just remember the slow deep breathing and the holding of our breath for only a few seconds and then breathing back out again. After a period of time we will start to see swirling rays of different colours. Some may see light, we may even see light through a hole as if we are sitting in a dark cave. We are all going to see and experience different things, no two people can see the same thing at the same time. As we will all have different experiences at different times, but that is okay as we are not in a race. So, we should be able to take our time.

If we choose to, we can even play some relaxing music that feels good for us, if it helps us to relax and to drift into relaxation and blissful comfort. Remember we are not going anywhere, as we are still in our bodies and just like waking up from our sleep we are in control. So, we can open our eyes slowly at any time if we wish to do so. Always remember to do it very slowly. Do we know that each and every one of us has a guide, from birth until we take our last breath? They are with us at all times on standby to help and guide us. They will only ever intervene when we ask them to, or to protect us during meditation if we are in need of that extra reassurance.

We are beginning to feel so relaxed and comfortable. The mind is getting weaker due to us keep pushing our thoughts out because all we want to do is to take slow deep breaths and feel so comfortable. So, that for the first time in our lives we are in tune with our inner selves. We begin to see colours or light, eventually as time goes on we will begin to see an eyeball. That is what's called the 'third eye'. As we call it our 'sixth sense'.

We live our day to day life using our two eyes but, once we are able to tune in with our higher soul, our soul sees only with the sixth sense. So, once we begin to see the eyeball we know that our sixth senses are beginning to work together with us. From that moment on our guides will be able to communicate with us, within ourselves. There will be many times when we will feel that it is only our thoughts, yes that is so right it will be our thoughts. Thoughts are only one, thoughts are energy and thoughts also become actions. When our thoughts begin to communicate with us once we have started to meditate a lot of people call that psychic. The reality is that we are in tune with our inner higher self, and only then we become one as some call it whole.

Another meditation when we wish to change someone else's feeling towards us into a more thoughtful loving feeling is to imagine pink light coming from out of our hearts and going into the other person's heart. Do that as often as you can, then watch that person's attitude and behaviour change towards you.

There may come times in our lives when we physically want to break the ties that bind us to other people. The great patron Saint of Protection Michael the Archangel is the divine celestial being with whom you need to work with for this. Imagine and familiarise yourself with his meditation. Begin to imagine that there is a silver cord going from our belly button to the belly button of those in our thoughts with whom you want to detach and cut away. Imagine the mighty fire sword of the magnificent Saint Michael cutting the cords that are currently linking or latched into the other person in your meditation. Now, we are no longer attached to that person spend a few moments and visualise Michael the Archangel healing the exposed cords, sealing them and protecting you. So, we have released that person and ourselves, and are no longer connected with our emotions.

When we are in the presence of anyone whom we feel needs to be calmed down, imagine pink light coming from the universe into their crown chakra (top of the head) and filling their whole body with a blue/ turquoise light. After a while, that person should begin to calm down.

Similar techniques can be used when cleansing our homes. Imagine white light coming from the universe in through the roof of our homes filling each and every corner of our homes all the way throughout our garden. Then watch that light going into a drain and disappearing into the drain, leaving our homes blessed and cleansed.

Chapter Four

Resentment is neither good for our way of living or for our health. Especially when it comes to our spirituality as it can stop our spiritual growth. Forgiveness is the most powerful tool for us to be able to proceed on such a path in life. By forgiving others is a way for us to release ourselves from situations and circumstances that physically tie us down. We can't move back or forth until we can learn to say 'I forgive you' and send our love out, actually meaning it from the bottom of our hearts. Those tender and loving words unlock our physical lock that may have had us chained to thoughts and people for years without us realising it. Always remember thoughts become actions. It is so very important to keep good thoughts in our heads, hearts and mind. Even our tongue should only speak good things otherwise it is better for us to remain quiet and silent.

No words are better than words that will cause harm to us and to the next person involved. It is easy for us to see faults in others for the downfalls we may have had in our lives, which in reality was all down to us. After all, if we have made our decisions then no matter what the outcome is then why can we not accept the outcome? Why do we always expect wonderful and good things to happen each and every time? How will we ever learn or develop our spiritual growth? We have to be able to accept the good with the bad. The quicker we can learn to live our lives in this manner, only then will our lives become easier and easier. Of course, we are still going to get our fair share of sad and hard times, but we learn to accept anything and everything. We learn to deal with it and then move on waiting for the next hurdle in life.

Life is full of ups and downs; we will have good, bad and sad times. There will be times where we will make others cry and others will make us cry. Unfortunately, all this is the reality of our everyday life. The only tools that can make changes in us are by trying to change in the way we act, behave and speak. Most importantly we need to be selective in the company that we keep. 'Tell me the company you keep and I will tell you what sort of a person you are', is the saying of my master. No matter how strong willed we may be, unless we mix in with good like-minded company we can easily become involved with being in the wrong place at the wrong time. There is a saying 'we can't choose our relatives, but thank God we can choose our friends'. Before we come onto this earth we have already chosen the people we want in our lives as they are the ones that teach us how to develop and learn. Yes, we did choose our own families and friends but, for some reason some may already know this. There are many of us that are not even aware of this.

Life is all about caring and sharing, giving and forgiving. We have turned our pure spiritual love into selfish love. Instead our love should only be selfless and unconditional. Most of us have become so selfish and inconsiderate that our ego won't let us identify our real inner self. There have been so many times in our lives when we have allowed other people to become closer to us, thinking that their feelings and intentions were similar to those that we had towards them. Their behaviour and actions had built such a good, kind and respectable image in our thoughts. There may be other times when we have got hurt as time has passed, the image that we had of the other person at the start is no longer there. This is because the other person led us to believe whatever they wanted us to believe and see, as their intentions were only based on selfish and conditional relationship. From the start they let us believe their intentions and love for us was unconditional and selfless.

Consider the scenario where Paul meets Becca, he knew she was new to the surroundings. He thought the only way he was able to win Becca's trust and friendship was to show her an image of what a caring, considerate and thoughtful being he was. There were many ways he did this, by intervening with her daily life and always being there every time she was in need of help. He wanted her to become dependent on him although he was doing it all for his own needy thoughts.

Becca only had to think of an idea and he would always be there to make it happen. There came a time when Paul began to get impatient as he had been doing all this running around for her to fall in love with him. She clearly wasn't showing any signs of having the same feelings towards him as her love for him was unconditional and pure. One day when he had enough and couldn't wait any longer he told Becca of his feelings towards her. She was quite taken back as it was not expected. She thought everything Paul had done for her was from the goodness of his heart. Becca had only ever seen him as a friend who was kind hearted, considerate and never thought of anything beyond that.

Becca tried to explain to Paul that yes, she did love him but only as her best friend. Paul said he had always wanted more than just her friendship, which is why he had done so much for her. Becca asked Paul to explain to her what the difference was between the love she had for him to the love he had for her. Instead of explaining, he started screaming and shouting that he had done this and that and that if it hadn't been for him she wouldn't be in the position that she was.

That was the first time Becca began to see just how selfish and conditional Paul's love towards her had been, and yet her love for him had been very genuine, pure and everlasting. A friendship can last forever whilst a relationship based on lust will only last for so long. That is why the company that we keep is so very important. We have to be able to see beyond what other people show us of themselves as every ones intentions are so different because we all want to live our lives in different ways and means. There are people who like to live their lives only for themselves and others who are happy to live their lives for others.

Reasons as to why we should help other people. It does not have to cost us more than our normal expenditure. We certainly don't have to stretch ourselves out too much, only as far enough to how much we feel comfortable with. That way, it will make no difference to our purse or to our every day routine. It may just be a slight change or adjustment. That way we will also benefit as we are expanding ourselves with our thoughts, heart, feelings and consideration. Every day our hands will slowly become helping hands, "the hands that help are holier than the lips that pray". We may even begin to see a more frequent smile on our faces without having to make that extra effort ourselves.

Imagine someone walking up to us, putting their arms around us or putting their hands together and saying 'thank you' to us. It automatically changes the whole form of our body and our reaction completely. Sometimes, those few seconds make us feel so small within ourselves as the other person involved is trying to express their gratitude. It sends a shiver through our body. Everything that happens, happens inside of us; other than the smile on our face as we say 'it was my pleasure' or 'the pleasure was all mine'. Some may even say 'we are only instruments for the Universe to be able to work through us'.

That way we begin to use the whole of our body, otherwise we are only functioning a portion at a time. We forget that our internal body is also awake and alive waiting for us to appreciate our inner body as well as our outer body. Each and every day we are mainly focusing on our outer body, our hair, skin, complexion, make up and the shape of our body as the list goes on and on. There are a lot of people who want to become a size zero that they push their bodies to such limits without realising that they are depriving their own body of all the things that the body needs to be able to function and remain strong and healthy.

So, we can't be the master of our minds but we can become the big masters of our body, deciding what we should be feeding it on or how much quantity we should be letting our bodies have. We push and push our bodies to such limits that when our bodies start to cry out for help. We still refuse to listen until the body through lack of nourishment can no longer carry us in our daily routines. Even then we run to the doctors or to the hospital and instead of feeding it with the foods it needs, we start filling ourselves with the medication given to us. That is why it is so very important to get in tuned with our inner selves, we need to listen and communicate with our inner voices and to every cell, bone, tissue and organs that help us to be who and what we really are.

Only then can we slowly start to recognise our real personalities. Throughout all of our lives we don't even know who or what we really are. Why do we occasionally question ourselves that something is lacking? We just cannot put a finger on what it is that is missing. We say 'oh I don't know what it is, but something is missing from my life'. Yes, something is missing but that what is missing is taking place inside of us not on the outside of us. That soul of ours that becomes our conscience as soon as we become attached to our bodies, is the real you, and I.

Only our conscience will teach us to recognise our real self. The sooner we can try to sit for a few minutes in silence, and then let the conscience pour out our real personalities. All we have to do is listen. We get so busy ordering and commanding that we forget that most times we also need to listen to our inner voice, our conscience that in reality is our soul (Atma), and only the soul is you or I. Why is so much happening all around us, all the destroying of the world, killings, stealing, robberies, drugs and alcohol? It is all happening because we refuse to listen to our conscience.

The conscience is the real master of us. If we just try and listen to our conscience it will try and talk to us and tell us not to do this or say that. Many times without thinking we know that we have hurt someone or another because of the existence of our ego and pride. Soon as we are on our own we begin to repent deep inside of ourselves, we begin to know just how wrong we were. It is then that guilt starts to overtake and we begin to feel terrible, although we may want to pick up the phone to say 'sorry' our ego and pride just won't let us do it.

Chapter Five

How can we call ourselves human? When we are so full of jealousy, ego and pride! We can't say that little word 'sorry' that can diffuse anything and make it vanish. All because of that little word 'sorry' a five-letter word, when spoken from our mouth becomes a strong commanding word. That no matter how annoyed the other party may be that simple sorry puts an end to a dispute. Instead of having wars in the world and destroying Mother Earth we need to have a war with ourselves. So, we can kill our ego, pride and jealousy that can break or even destroy us. We could have the most fantastic personality, but these three things over shadow our real personalities that we find it so hard to say sorry. Like Elton John's song 'Sorry seems to be the hardest word'. If we feel that we are always right and only the other person around us is wrong then we have not given our conscience a chance to have birth within ourselves. This is because there isn't anyone on this earth who can always be right and others wrong.

A person can only call themselves a human being when they listen to their conscience and let their conscience be the master of them. It is only then we can honestly say that 'I am the master of my mind'. Yes, we should all be living our lives being the masters of our own minds. In order for us to enable ourselves to be the master of our minds we have to let our conscience guide us every minute of the day. Only then we will be complete, because that is the only time when our heart, thoughts, feelings and actions begin to all function together.

We are human beings. Do we really know how we actually work? Scientists are always busy trying to find out this and that but even they are unable to understand things that lie inside each and every one of us. Have scientists been able to discover just where our soul goes to when it leaves our rented bodies, or where it comes from as it enters a mother's womb? Have they been able to discover at what stage of a baby being inside of a mother's womb does the soul enter the baby's body? There are so many things that even we don't know about ourselves, and we can spend our whole lives and still never get to know the real us.

Yet, just because we have a pair of outer eyes we feel and think we know everything and about everyone. If we were stuck inside of a dark cave and looked out, can we honestly say that we can see everything that is outside just by looking through a small hole? No, we would only be able to see a portion of that space that only the hole will allow us to see. We have no clue of the rest. How can we judge on something that we can't even see?

Do we honestly know who and what we are? We can sit for hours and hours trying to find the answer. Am I the mind? The answer is No, because we are not the mind. Am I the body? The answer is No as we are not the body. We are only linked with our bodies but should learn to detach ourselves so that the body and the conscience, which is the soul, should be separated. We should be totally separated from our bodies, for we as a soul are not the body, mind or senses.

Each time we walk into our homes, that we live in most of the time, we are still separated from our place of residence. As we walk all day long walking from room to room we know that our homes are our shell of comforts, separated from ourselves. The same feelings and understanding should be about our souls and bodies. We should be totally separated from our bodies for we are not the body or the mind. The more we realise this form of truth the more we will begin to experience that no aches, pains or illness can touch us because all these things are linked only to the body and nothing can reach our souls. So we should be able to live our lives in peace and bliss.

The only existence on this earth is love and we are not just talking about love that is linked to lust as that kind of love is not eternal. It only lasts for a short period of time. Only pure love is divine and that sort of unconditional love can be everlasting. To love others is to love ourselves. If we have not learnt to love ourselves then how can we possibly love another? To love ourselves we need to know everything about ourselves, away from our body, mind and senses. We need to know our real inner selves which is the soul

(Atma). The most important issues in our lives are that we don't learn to love ourselves. That prevents us from loving others around us.

It could be neighbours, friends, family or anyone else in our lives. How can we love others when we don't even know what love is ourselves? We are not who we think we are, or the person that others think we are. Realistically we don't know who and what we are. Our senses and desires stop us from getting to know our real inner selves. We have become so mean and selfish that our lives become all me and mine. Our minds start to fill up with ego, jealousy and pride and all the negative thoughts that can cause harm and destroy us. We are quite capable of destroying ourselves by becoming our own worst enemy. Where there is love and true honest pure love there can be no room for anything else.

Different people abuse their money in different ways. We human beings don't realise just how wrong it is to waste time and money. We spend so much time searching for worldly needs and desires. We spend every moment of the day focusing so much on our needs that we forget that time is so precious. One day soon we will leave all these worldly possessions behind as we leave everything and everyone behind as we move forward onto our different journeys. Only then we realise just how much of that wasted time was spent on worrying, needing and yearning that could have been enjoyed by us with our loved ones. So, let's not waste even a moment looking for this and that.

Problems are mainly created by us. They happen due to our own negligence or the company that we did not keep that was like-minded to our own ways and habits. How many times do we mix with other people who have no idea of who and what we really are? They only see us from their own thinking concept, and we have no idea of what sort of an image they have of us. Wouldn't it be great if that image of ourselves could pop up in front of ourselves so that we too could see for ourselves, how others see us?

It is very rare if we are lucky and fortunate enough to get others to see the good qualities in us. We can bring six people into our minds who we feel know us well enough and if we ask those six people to write down a dozen things as to how they see us. I am sure that those six people will write so many different things about us to one another. Some of those qualities that they see in us may not even be true, but it's exactly how they see us. If we stood in front of a blind person and asked them to describe what we are wearing, would a blind person be able to do that?

The same thing happens with the people in our everyday life. When we are running around pleasing others, we are great and wonderful. As soon as we are not able to please them, then they see us as not being so wonderful. Try and see it for yourselves, how people's opinions towards us change as soon as we stop pleasing them. We don't realise how we have become their servants, their wish has become our command as all we do is please them until there comes a day when we can't please them anymore. Only our soul (Atma) can help us to see the truth and reality in each and every one of us.

If we have no expectations then we would only see one personality in our loved ones. Instead we see one person change into so many different people due to our own needs, greed and selfish desires. Yes, we are very selfish; it all seems to be about our needs and desires. Those wants and wants, give me give me. We need to change our behaviour and thinking concept towards others. First of all, we need to learn to love ourselves, our inner selves which is our soul. Only then can we learn to love and have respect for others. Love and respect should play a very important role in our everyday life.

We say we love them and them but have we asked ourselves, 'Do we really love them?' When we haven't discovered what love really is. Love can only be experienced with our hearts, and never by anything else. Some people try and love others with their heads, that sort of love is very conditional. The head will only let you love the other person from a business point of view. You will love that person until you have gained whatever your search in that relationship was. As soon as that person has given us all they had to give, we soon get fed up of them and to top it off we even have the audacity to blame them for the reasons as to why we don't want them to be a part of our lives any longer.

Want is so different to need. Want is very demanding. So, whenever we want this and that all we are doing is demanding our wants. Whenever we feel we have the need that then becomes a requirement, can we not change our behaviour from always demanding to need and require? Let's also try and stop our selfish motive minds from using and abusing others in our lives. Let's learn to have respect for others, and only then will others have respect for us. Remember we have to gain their respect by being kind, considerate, honest and truthful.

There must have been someone or another we may all have used and abused at some point in our lives. When the great Divine Universe is so good and kind to send that special person into our lives then that person who tries so hard to put a smile on our faces, and due to our selfish personalities, it never seems to happen. That person is always giving and never expects anything in return. All they wish to see is that we are happy and even then we don't know what happiness really is, because the more they give us, the more we want. If they give us an inch we want a yard, and if, they give us a finger we want their hand.

It's all want, want, want, and demand until the day comes that we have taken all that there was to be taken. So, what do we do? Instead of appreciating their kindness and considerate friendship we knock off their self-esteem by labelling them with horrible things. We blame them for the wrong in our life and most of the wrong are only in our minds. What right do we have to use anyone in our life or to abuse them? Life should be about giving and taking, sharing and caring. Would it really hurt us to say 'thank you' and 'I love you'? If we are able to learn how to say 'I love you' it can change us as a person. I don't mean the selfish love, but the selfless love, where there are no conditions or expectations.

Chapter Six

I would like to meet the person who invented money. Why can we not live our lives if there was no money involved? Only love, peace and consideration. If we all worked hard in the way that we do then would we really need money? I know people say 'money is what makes the world go round' but does it? Like I said if we all worked with honesty then we wouldn't need money.

I would do anything to make this world a better, loving, peaceful, kind and considerate place for us to live in. Where all we could see was good laughter and happiness. People abuse money in different ways. Some spend and it still brings them no peace or contentment in their lives as real happiness is already inside of them. They just don't know this and are so busy searching for that peace and happiness on the outside of this world. Yes, we can find happiness on the outside as well, but at first we have to change in our behaviour, attitude and way of life. It is only then that we can start living for one another, in peace, bliss and harmony.

Many people gamble thousands of their wealth away. They may have gained their wealth that may have been passed down to them from their wealthy relatives, because it may have come easily to them 'easy come, easy go'. They don't know what it's like to have worked hard, through hard effort and sweat to have earned and saved. So, they blow it very easily without having any consideration because they didn't have to work hard for it. It was easy money that came easy and so much of it that not everyone is able to handle life with too much money. So they turn to sex, gambling, drugs and alcohol. Do we actually need any of these things?

Do we need drugs? What do we gain from taking them? Why gamble, and throw away hard earned money? These people are so lucky and blessed souls to have gained all that wealth. Wouldn't it be wonderful instead of wasting that money, if they could help the less fortunate souls? Help them gain education, good health or put food in their stomach. We are all aware of all that is happening in this world that we are living in. So what are our excuses not to be able to help one another at a time of need? We can blow our money on ourselves and our families, on things that we don't even need or require, but our spending continues endlessly.

We don't have to let go of our wealth, only a few pence or pounds that will make a lot of difference to other people. A few pence put together by a few people can put a little food in someone's mouth or buy school books in a place where there are no schools so that these children are able to learn how to read and write. We can all do so much together if only we can put our hands into our pockets and pull out a few pence. There are so many countries that need our love, help, support, food, clothes and medicine.

Does it not bring a tear to our eyes or break our hearts that so much is happening in the world, where people have lost their loved ones, possessions and homes through no fault of their own? Yet, we may have millions and billions just sitting in our banks or homes. That a few pence or pounds from that can change some one's life, and when we die is that money going to go with us? How much money do we or our family really need to live on?

Yes, we may have worked so very hard to earn our money. What is the point of having ten cars or five homes if we can't help our brothers and sisters who are so desperately in need of our help and support?

If this happens to us with tsunami floods or earthquakes, then what will happen to our wealth, money, gold etc.? I have been trying to explain to the people around me that there may come a day where we may face a shortage of food. If that happens we must share our food with our neighbours, it is better to eat a little less and share our food with others.

We have become so selfish and mean living in this world that every day is becoming materialistic. All that most people want from life is control and power, whether it is in politics or over our family and friends. What is it that we are trying to gain, power and control over? How many people are losing their happiness, peace and some even their lives because of this? We are the ones who are destroying this world that we live in, which we have been blessed with. There is nothing in this world that belongs to us even our relatives and friends are not ours. As people should not be considered as possessions. The truth is that nothing and no one belongs to us not even our bodies. Only our soul that lives within us is forever eternal.

62

Chapter Seven

My own experiences have very much shaped the person I am today. Some things I have been blessed to witness and some things have deeply shocked me but nevertheless it was all part of my soul purpose and life experience. These experiences have allowed me to challenge and build my own thinking concepts to better myself very much as I've described and encouraged you to do. I will now share some of that light in the form of my experiences with you.

As a frequent traveller to India I usually tend to go and stay in Juhu (Mumbai). I feel that it is my second home, as I enjoy taking a walk along Juhu beach in the evenings. As for me, that is a time when you see a different variety of people, some are poor who bring their food from home and they will sit on the beach as a family having their meal together. Then there are others who may be middle class who are able to buy their food from the Chapatti Beach food stalls. India is a place where different spectrums of extremes exist; either you are from a family in the lower class or upper class. You won't often find many people who are from the middle class as the gap between the extremes due to the current recession keeps widening. It touched my heart when I walked on the beach and saw the poorest of the poor still offer and say 'come and join us, and have a meal with us'. I always thank them for the offer, and explain that I am very touched but I have already eaten. Always should a person show humility and gratitude to those that offer to people despite having less and still having the great heart to share.

For me, there is no high or low class or any creed. We are all the same as we came into this world the same way and the souls go out the same way when leaving this earthly plane. Money is not significant. In fact one can be richer with one's good heart. Money comes and goes, morality comes and grows. Whenever we go to Santa Cruz there are a few places where I go to eat. Whilst I've stood there eating, it's a guarantee as it is in most parts of poverty filled areas that a few beggars will approach us asking for money. As I don't like giving money to them, in case that money is spent on drugs and alcohol or on the wrong things, I usually buy them food that I know will benefit them. Or, I will take them into the grocery store and buy them the food that they may need (within reason).

I enjoy going to visit Mother Theresa's orphanages, where I have been going to since I first visited India. There is one orphanage where there are children who for some reason or another were not wanted; some children have been left on the doorstep. We will take books, toys and sometimes the nuns have even asked us for creams that we have taken from England. We usually ask the nuns what it is that they need and we will then go to the local stores there and buy them.

The other orphanage that we like to visit is where there are old people living as their families no longer want or are unable to take care of them. So, the old people are living there until their last days. It brings so much joy and tears visiting places like these. Tears to know how can other people treat their family or friends like this when we ourselves know that we too are going to be old, just like them (if we are able to live that long). A well-known saying comes to mind when I see how these elders have been treated, 'what goes around comes around'.

Children are so pure and innocent, how can anyone who has carried a child for nine months in their womb give them up? I am not judging anyone; I am only trying to understand how and why a mother can do this? It shows that we are all on a different level with our thinking concept. Children bring tears and joy into our lives and into our hearts. We also learn a lot from children as they are tomorrow's people. So, how we mould them is up to us. We lay the foundations for them in the way we act and behave in their presence. Children are a lot of hard work but at the same time they bring so much joy into our lives. We should teach our children discipline and how to love and respect.

Being able to spend time in Juhu, I get to see a lot of Bollywood film stars, some I have found to be very humble and there are others who forget who have put them in that position in the first place. Having time to smile or give an autograph is too much for them, but if it wasn't for the public that became their fans, believe me they would not be at that status or be able to earn the hefty amount of money that they do. This is due to the public listening to their music and watching their movies.

I watched a film star refusing to sign an autograph, the action that he took hurt my feelings and yet it wasn't I that wanted to have a picture or his autograph. It made no difference to me as he and I are just one. I really felt like holding onto his arm for even a few seconds and asking why he was being like this. Yes, we are all entitled to have an off day, but why take it out on someone who has taken their own time to appear somewhere just so that they are able to catch a glimpse of their idol.

His fan was not getting paid for being there, but turned up through the goodness of his heart and for the unconditional love he must have had for that idol of his. Look, how selfish and conditional the response was that he got in return from the superstar. Here was the fan giving his selfless and unconditional time, and yet in return he was getting nothing. He was just grateful for just that quick glimpse, after waiting hours. Yes, we can also say that his motive was to see the actor so somewhere along the line it may have been a little conditional.

If there are any celebrities reading this then I would like to make a request to them that please find it in your hearts to make a minor adjustment towards your fans. If they had no fans, who gave them time and attention then they would not be in the position that they are in. No matter how much time and effort they may have put into their hard work. Your fans are like God, without them you would not be able to call yourself an icon in the public eye. Without their time and effort you would not be where you are today.

Your fans expect no more than a little time for them. A little wave, smile or even a thank you is not a lot to give back in return for all that they have given to you. In life 'one has to give to gain something in return' (smile, love). Please try and have respect and love for all those people who have showered and graced you with their kind hearts and love. As the Indian saying goes 'to gain something one has to lose something else'.

Other people have to spend their time and money whether they go to the cinema to watch your movies or pay to buy your DVD to watch at home, or have taken their time to listen to your music. They may have paid a lot of money to buy your CD's. When people go to concerts again they spend a lot of their hard earned money, and have taken their own time to come and see you perform.

They may not have as much money as you, but even their time is valuable where no price tag can ever be put on time. As time is one thing that money just cannot buy. It is the same with real pure love, money cannot buy love but a true heart can win love over. Not buy it! Win love over! Where there is love there is peace, where there is peace there is harmony, where there is harmony there is trust, where there is trust there is divinity.

I have been a fan of Oprah Winfrey for many years and I can truly say that she is an idol for me. I could sit in front of the TV for hours and watch her shows. She does so much for others with so much dedication. She has never looked at her own bank balance but she wants to make a difference to other people's lives.

I can openly admit that there have been times when I have sat, watched her shows and thought she is in the form of a goddess. If I was ever fortunate to be able to meet her, I would bow down in respect for all the good she has done for others. I have learnt so much from her over the years and can honestly say that she plays a big part in me being the person that I am today. I will always look up to Oprah Winfrey as my Ustaad (teacher).

Deepak Chopra is another person who has been a very big inspiration to me. You can see the inner peace within him just from the glow on his face. He is an individual who is in control of his thoughts and knows who and what he is. There have been a couple of occasions when I have been to visit Deepak and for some reason it has not been possible. Once, was several years ago at a Heart and Soul exhibition, I had missed him by an hour or so and the other time was whilst I was in Delhi. He had left the city the day before I had arrived. It was quite unfortunate and disappointing that I wasn't able to meet him but, I know that when the universe thinks it's time, our paths will cross.

Another celebrity that comes in my mind is Cheryl Cole. A lot of people misjudge her as they forget that she is still quite young. I think a lot is expected from her in the public eye and people don't really see her for who and what she is. She has touched the hearts of so many people. She is also a legend that is an inspiration to so many people. To me she is an angel in disguise and doesn't get the credit that she truly deserves. Cheryl Cole is a people's person and does genuinely care for the people around her, whether it's family or the public that have supported her.

Apart from the three people I have mentioned there are many others who are good human beings and have had so much to give. Celine Dion is another person that gives out some much healing to a lot of people through her singing. I have heard and spoken with a lot of people who have felt that healing takes place in their bodies through listening to her music. Look at David Beckham. His heart is always in search of little children who may be suffering, his feet and legs may be on a football pitch, but his hands are always out helping someone or other who is in need. We are fortunate to be living in a world alongside these people. But, how often do we stop and appreciate them or actually recognise the good in others? The answer is, we don't! Instead we are always expecting more from them. We are so engrossed in always wanting that we often forget to give. Life should be about 'caring and sharing', 'giving and taking'.

Chapter Eight

Let's all spread a little more pure love into other people's hearts and to the rest of the world. So, that the world we are all living in begins to shine bright with all our love. Let's all be good and kind towards each other. This world Mother Earth we call Dharti Maa to feel that kind of love. Mother Earth can only experience that love through us. We don't need to call anyone our enemies because we are all one. We are all brothers and sisters, and yes one big family.

We may be different colours, come from different backgrounds or speak different languages but love only has one language. That language comes from the heart and we don't need to speak love we just need to feel love. Open our hearts wide and let the language of love flow in and out of our hearts. Once the love starts to flow in and out of our hearts, our little hearts will expand into big, kind hearted loving hearts.

The truth is that we may have many different countries but, there is only one language and that is the language of the heart called love. The day we arrive in to this world, we come with nothing. We don't even have a name and that is given to us only after we are born. We come into this world without an identity. How much more proof does our monkey mind require that we come into this world all naked, empty-handed and without anything? Yet, we leave with nothing as our body and our name all remain on this earth. It is only our soul that once arrived on its own with nothing, will depart again all alone with nothing. Therefore, we are not the body or the mind. We are only the conscience (Atma, the soul).

I pledge my heart out to each and every one of you and plead with you to learn to love one another. Without love there is not anything else that is priceless as love. Love is free as it is not sold on the market, love cannot be bought as it has no price. Love is priceless and very precious; it grows free of charge in our hearts. I hope some people will begin to change some of their behaviour, as it costs nothing to give someone a smile (it also gives us the opportunity to show off our teeth).

We should try and be more humble, throw ego out of our lives as we don't need ego in our lives. We can wake up one morning and lose everything so we should not take anything for granted. If anything, we should be blessed with what we have and the people we have in our lives.

Pride, ego and jealousy are the three things I keep well out of my body as my body is the temple of a living God. These three things are what can change my personality within the click of a finger. I am so blessed to have my health which to me is my wealth. I am so lucky that I get to sleep in my comfortable bed and that I get enough food to eat when my body needs it. I think every morning how well Mother Earth looks after my welfare, and from the bottom of my heart I thank Mother Earth for what I have been provided with for my every day needs. Each and every one of us has been so blessed with so much that we forget to appreciate and show gratitude.

Why can we not all live our lives in pure peace and harmony, put an end to all the violence that is taking place all around us. We should put our arms around each other and embrace everyone around us. We are on this earth for a short period of time, so why not make the most of the time that is left. Believe me, our lives are so very short, a lot shorter than we could imagine. That is why it is so very important to learn to laugh, smile and be happy. We should bring the tears of joy into our own and the eyes of our loved ones.

We should be living for this very moment for tomorrow may never come. Our lives should be of total bliss and peace, there should be nothing or no one who should be able to take the smile off our face. We should be able to turn our homes into heaven and expand our hearts to be even bigger. There is no limit to how big we want our hearts to become. All we need to do is keep reminding ourselves this is about love, love and total blissful love.

We should love our bodies and soul over again and again. It is only then that we can start to reflect through others around us. Watch and see our love begin to light up the whole world. At the moment we are living in a world where there is total darkness and love can lighten up every ones lives so that the world that we live in can once again start to light up and shine love and peace.

Our soul is no more than a light. We can call it a flicker of a light or a tiny Christmas light. We should ask ourselves that if we are all the lights then why is there so much darkness in our lives, homes and in the world? It is all down to us because of our own negativity which has been created by our greedy, selfish and jealous monkey minds. Instead, we are in a position to be able to turn all that negativity around into positive action. This is where each and every one can benefit from them. We are tearing ourselves apart and to do this we don't need any help from anyone else as we are quite capable of doing it ourselves.

Why are we punishing ourselves? Why can we not reverse everything into peace, love and harmony? Love is eternal. Why did the universe give us a heart? It wasn't given to us to break. It was given to us to mend. When someone breathes their last breath it is always the heart that stops beating first. The rest of our organs may still be able to function for a little longer until they shut down. Our soul is what works with the heart.

Our conscience is not able to work for us all by itself. How many times do we underestimate our hearts? We are so used to thinking that we operate with our brain and mind. What about the thoughts and feelings that are linked with our hearts. There are so many different things that we can do with our bodies but each and every one of our organs are only able to do one thing. Our heart was only created to love, so where did resentment and hate come from? Look how our heart pumps blood all through our body, our blood is red so is the colour of love.

Let's all fill our bodies with pink light and send that pink light out to each and every one so that the world we live in gets filled with lots of love. The war, hate and resentment become something of the past. We cannot do anything about the past as it has already happened but we can still change the future of the world by filling our hearts with so much joy and love. War and resentment has never gained anything, where love and peace can rule the whole world.

Power is only a word that exists in a few people's minds; thank God that not everyone is in search of power. Does anyone really know what power actually is, or what does power gain for us?

This word power has destroyed the world we live in and has taken many lives of people through no fault of their own. We need to put an end to war, the destruction of the world and the lives of innocent people who are not even ready to leave so many loved ones behind. Yes, we ourselves can put an end to war by making our hearts expand even bigger. Our heart is the biggest weapon this world or scientists could ever create. Only our hearts can put an end to these killings that are taking place every second somewhere or another.

There is absolutely nothing that belongs to us in this world, and so we must come to realise this truth, the better it would be for us. We then need to ask ourselves if nothing belongs to us then what it is that we are fighting for. For heaven's sake, even the time we live on is not ours, as each and every one is again as I keep repeating is living on borrowed time. Our dirty, filthy, cruel monkey mind has buried and destroyed our good health. We say 'I am not well, this and that is wrong with me', but in fact we are our own worst enemy. We don't need any help from anyone else for we are quite capable of destroying ourselves and that is exactly what we are doing. We are destroying our bodies that are meant to be loaned to us, as temples of a living God.

We are also destroying the world that we should be living in. We are killing, polluting and destroying everything around us, that we have forgotten words like kindness, peace, love, forgiveness, care, share and cherish. We cannot even be bothered to use our hearts to love one another but, we can use weapons like guns, bombs and knives to kill one another.

Why, oh why, are we becoming so unkind and cruel? Is that the only reason we were put on this earth? So that we can destroy Mother Earth, be ungrateful and inconsiderate. Then what are we going to teach our children, if we are acting and behaving in this selfish, cruel and inconsiderate manner? We should be ashamed of ourselves and call ourselves nothing. What have we learnt, nothing? But, we have learnt to run for name and fame, power, sex, drugs, alcohol, money and lots more money! Does it matter whether we kill, steal, lie or cheat to gain that power and money? Hey, it's only someone's life that we have taken! Does it really matter?

All the time that I was growing up again and again I would hear how politics and religion are two things one should never talk about. As so many disputes and debates can arise, no one ever said that one could not be spiritual or to lend a helping hand unconditionally without expecting anything in return. This is because they cared and wanted to help through the goodness of their hearts. Today, there is nobody who wants to buy you a cup of tea or coffee without expecting something in return.

If we sat down and took only a moment to face facts, the truth of the matter is that NOTHING is ours. For what are we proud of that makes us full of pride, ego and jealousy? We are nothing; we are no one that is why that when we are born we are born with nothing. We come into the world naked with no clothes not even a tag with a name on it. We don't even have a name that we have to be named only after we enter into this selfish, cruel and materialistic world, a world that can be changed into a wonderful, loving and peaceful world. It could be filled with lots of love, caring and sharing.

I will say again and again each and every moment of the day that nothing belongs to us whilst we are on this earth. So what are we fighting for? We don't even own the body that our soul is living in. There will come a day when our soul which is our conscience that we have locked and thrown the key away will leave our rental bodies. The body will be placed in a coffin to be buried or cremated and our soul will wave goodbye and go back to its home. We have all come into this world only to learn our lessons.

How can we learn anything when we are so busy destroying one another? We go to temples, mosques and church etc., what do we actually learn from going there? All of our paths are the same only the teachings are different. They all teach us that we are all one and have to love and help one another. Even though we are all one, we have chosen to be separate from one another because of our selfish, egoistic monkey minds.

The word 'respect' is beginning to fade away as we no longer have respect for ourselves let alone having respect for anyone else. We have 'I couldn't care less' attitude. Why are we beginning to crumble as human beings by becoming animals? Even animals have more consideration for each other than we as human beings do. We have alarms, cameras and no end of locks on our doors, why? It is because we no longer feel safe in our own homes, and we don't even realise that it's our own doings.

Chapter Nine

How safe is it to be able to walk all alone in the middle of the night? What has this world become, where one human being is scared and frightened of another? So, how can we say that we are all one and belong together? Yet, animals can wonder around anywhere and at any time of the day. Now what does that tell us? It tells us that we humans can no longer walk about but the animals can. We have become prisoners in our homes and in the world that we are supposed to be living in.

What gives us the right to take something that belongs to another when it clearly tells us in the Bible 'thou shall not steal'. What gives us the right to kill and take someone else's life when again it says 'thou shall not kill'. In fact we are doing almost the opposite of what our spiritual paths have forbidden us to do. We are not worthy of being called human beings. We have become robbers of our own souls;

we have forgotten the reasons as to why we have been blessed with such beautiful bodies and good health which is our wealth. We have been blessed with homes, cars and everything we could possibly need and want.

Yet, we are still not happy and content. We are always crying out for more. We don't even know what it is that we are searching for? Real happiness and contentment lies within each and every one of us. So, why are we searching near and far? If we are not happy and content then how can materialistic things possibly bring us happiness? Why should we not be happy, we are so blessed and lucky souls? What more do we really need, we have got our health? We should remember that there is always someone out there who is less fortunate than ourselves.

We can see, but what about the ones who are blind? We can hear but what about the ones who are deaf? We can walk but what about the ones who have no legs and feet to be able to walk with? Our health is our wealth. We don't need alcohol or drugs to be able to live our lives in peace and harmony.

In fact if these two things are not controlled then it can lead to grief, heartache and pain. We can lose ourselves and our loved ones due to drugs and alcohol. These two things can make us do almost anything out of character and get us in to some serious trouble and kill us. If we don't seek help and put a stop to it then they will put an end to us.

We have all heard of Noah's Ark. Look how Noah was asked to put all the animals on the boat two by two as the rest of the world came to an end. If we don't change our habits, ways and attitude then one day very soon the same thing is going to happen to us and I don't think any of us are going to become Noah and build an ark. How can anyone save us when we are doing all this to ourselves and the world that we are living in?

Mother Earth must be sick and tired of our cruel and selfish behaviour not only towards her but even towards ourselves. We can change and put a stop to all this nonsense just like that. We don't need any tools. All we need to do is to stop killing, destroying, hating and resenting one another.

We can change all this. Love one another by lending a helping hand, to share our food and thoughts with the less fortunate ones, give away a few clothes that we no longer wear and won't miss them.

Look around our gardens for the garden tools we no longer use or need and send them to places or countries where people are so dependent on those tools. Those tools could be used to grow and put food in their mouths. There is so much we can do to help our brothers and sisters in other parts of the world. There could be things that are just sitting in our homes, offices, garden or garden sheds that could help another person get by in life.

Instead of wasting time sending resentment and bad thoughts to those who may have hurt us let's send out good, happy and positive thoughts and love out into the world. Especially to those who are suffering at this moment in time as they may have lost their homes and loved ones through the natural disasters that are happening today.

We can do so much sitting in our offices, cars and homes without lifting a finger. We only have to send out loving thoughts as those thoughts become actions. Let's take a few seconds to pray for the sick people who are suffering somewhere in this big wide world, let's thank our loved ones for being in our lives and making our lives worth living. We should thank each and every organ in our bodies for taking good care of us. If it wasn't for our bodies functioning properly then what would happen to our souls.

Take a look out of the window and at the world that the Great Universe has blessed us with. We have got so much to live for as the world is our oyster, nothing is impossible and we can do anything as long as we put our hands and mind to it. So, please let's start living our lives and I mean actually living our lives in peace and harmony. We can do this by making ourselves and the others around us laugh, which doesn't even cost us anything. Laughter is a great healer for a sick body and mind. Try laughing and smiling and see what happens. Watch someone else smile. Watch the change that laughter will make to our lives. We have forgotten what it is like to smile by being so serious most of the time.

Make changes right now, as it still isn't too late. How I wish I could make some changes to the world, to make it a great place to live in and with everyone's help we can make these changes and this is where this book comes into play. On our own we are only one, but when we come together we become a unity and that unity becomes divinity. We are all one but somewhere along the way we have all been separated but it still is not too late for us to all become one again. A saying that comes to mind is 'It's better late than never'.

We don't have to do much, even sending good thoughts, stop rushing around, and give another driver way whilst driving. Even a simple smile can help the next person by taking away their worries and problems. Let's hum and sing to ourselves even when our heart wants to cry out, make our heart smile and fill it with laughter and love. Tell our near and dear ones just how much they mean to us and how wonderful our world is by having them being a part of it. Our loved ones make life worth living for today as tomorrow may never come.

If we have elderly people living in our street go over and see if they need anything. It could be anything from getting them milk from the shop or just keeping them company for a while.

'Worship to man is worship to God'

'Hands that help are holier than the lips that pray'

'Help ever, hurt never'

Sathya Sai Baba

There is so much that we can do to make this world a better, friendlier, safer and happier place to live in. If we can help one another then a day will arrive when people won't need to steal what doesn't belong to them. Honesty and truth will play one of the most important parts in our lives. We won't be frightened or scared to take a walk all alone and will be able to see more elderly people walking about instead of them being locked away and scared in their own homes. They have become so scared and frightened of the society that we live in.

If everyone can learn to say no to drugs then people who sell them won't have any buyers and that can put an end to the crime and theft. Let them work for their living just like any of us who make a hard honest living through hard work and effort. Let's get up in the mornings and be very grateful for another glorious day as tomorrow may never come and we are fortunate enough to see yet another day.

Thank our pillow and bed in our homes, cars; thank the sun for making the world beautiful and brighter place for us to live in. Thank the whole planet, our family and friends and show them just how much they mean to us and how much we love them. Let's not forget to say our please and thank you, learn how to control our tempers by staying calm no matter what happens. Let's learn to lower the tone of our voice even if we so much want to scream and shout. Learn to think before we speak, learn to say the kind things and put away the unkind things.

We should thank our lucky stars for who and what we are, for our health is our wealth. Let's appreciate everything that we have in our lives and not just what we think suits us. Let's learn to express our inner selves and feelings. If we love someone let's tell them just how we feel and if someone has hurt us then let's tell them very politely that we didn't like what was said, done or how it was said and kindly ask them not to repeat that performance again. If they continue to do so then maybe it is time for us to wave our goodbyes to them and we may have to leave them behind as we may have learnt all we were meant to learn and now it's time for us to move on. There will always be a next person as our life is a learning experience.

Speaking the truth is very important but, if by speaking the truth will ruin, hurt or destroy someone then it is better to remain silent and say nothing (silence is golden, we all know that). We need to learn how to speak less and not talk for the sake of talking. Let's not waste time as time is so very precious, 'time waste, is life waste'. Sending out good thoughts and prayers is a must.

If we cannot say something good about someone or something then let's say nothing at all. See good in others as we have many faults in ourselves. Let's think before we start pointing fingers at others. Let's forget the good that we may have done for others and the harm others have done to us. Help others only unconditionally otherwise do nothing at all. Service to man is service to God.

Let's not chase and run after name and fame. What was our name before we came into this world? What will our name be as our soul leaves this world? Money comes and goes, morality comes and grows'. We need money to be able to survive to pay our bills and put food in our mouths. We need to decide just how much money we want and then compare it to how much we really need. We need to put some away for a rainy day. We don't need too much money as money can become like a shoe size. It has to be just right, for us to be able to get about quite comfortably. If it is too big or small it becomes uncomfortable so it has to be just right as a shoe size.

In spirituality it is said, 'if we have too much baggage then we cannot travel light'. So let's not collect too much baggage as one day we will have to leave everything behind, our soul leaves empty and all alone, in the same as it once came with nothing.

Nobody or nothing will be able to go with us when it is time for us to depart from this rental body of ours. No one has come on this earth to remain here for evermore.

Everything has a date on it; everything on this Earth comes to an end as time waits for nobody. Every second the clock is ticking away is bringing us closer and closer to our sell by date. When that day arrives we may not be with our loved ones and that is the one reason why we should love them, but at the same time learn to detach from them, as farewell is a lonely sound when said to someone we love.

We will have no choice. Our soul will leave our body and this life that we are living in as quickly as we blink our eyes. We will not be able to say our goodbyes. So, whether we like it or not, whether or not we want to accept it we should learn to detach ourselves from our material gains and from our loved ones as one day either they will leave us or we will leave them. Detachment does not mean that we love them any less or that we no longer will be there for them at times of need, it means that our possessive love becomes unconditional selfless love. We should live every moment knowing that a moment is about to arrive when we will depart from our rental bodies and from this life.

In reality life is no more real than our dreams that we have whilst sleeping. How real those dreams may seem, it is only when we wake up that we realise that they were only dreams. How real those dreams felt at the time. If they were good dreams we get disappointed that it was only a dream. If it had been an awful dream then we are so relieved to know it was only a bad dream. Well, this life of ours that we have got so engrossed into by making permanent fittings and fixtures is only a dream and one day soon we are going to wake up and all this life of ours and what is in it is no more than a dream.

There is nothing in this world that is real, not our mind, body, thoughts and senses. We are not the body or all these things, for we are the soul (Atma). We are neither the body, senses or mind that is why we need to be in control of our senses. Instead we let our senses and mind run around wild, our senses become a worldly desire that has no end...

unless we learn to control them. Once we have learnt to control our senses and mind, our thoughts will automatically be controlled. Then from that moment on our lives become so blissful that even our lifestyle will become simple, as our wisdom will take over.

We will become so in bliss with ourselves that no matter how much someone or the whole world stands in front of us and try to criticise us none of their insults will be able to reach us as we have been able to rearrange all of our paths and all that they will be doing is insulting our body. They have no idea about our soul. Now that our soul has detached from our body nothing or no one will be able to hurt us, as that was only happening to us whilst we were the body and we are now no longer the body, nothing should be able to affect us. All worldly links are connected only to the body and all spirituality is linked only to the soul which is our conscience.

Each and every one of us should be detached from our bodies for we are not the bodies, mind, senses or our thoughts. We are a very simple soul that has taken form of a human whilst we are on this earth and each and every one of us has come down on this earth to pay off our karma and to develop so that we can learn our lessons. Until we learn our lessons we are going to have to come back on earth again and again to meet the same souls until we decide to accept our reasons why we are here on earth and to do something about it.

To be able to do something about it is for us to make changes to the way we think, behave and live our lives. We need to be honest with ourselves and with others, we need to only speak the truth and be true to ourselves. We have to learn to be not violent towards anyone, we need to bring peace back into our lives so that peace then will begin to exist in the world that we are living in. Right conduct is another role that should be a part of our everyday living. We can adapt and learn to live with the five values of peace, truth, right conduct, non-violence and love. We can even do a few minutes meditation upon these five values and they will slowly sink into our way of living.

Chapter Ten

To be honest and truthful is a must otherwise how can we call ourselves a civilised human being, when we can't be honest to ourselves? There are many souls that can tell one lie after another and yet their conscience has not been allowed into their lives because once we have allowed consciousness into our lives we will not be allowed to tell a lie or be dishonest even if we wanted to.

Try and see it for yourself

Even a white lie will start to eat us up inside because we will keep on beating ourselves up as to why did we tell a lie, and why were we dishonest to ourselves? Yes, we are cheating and deceiving only ourselves by telling lies because we cannot even begin to be true and honest to ourselves. We need to have some respect for ourselves first before we can learn to respect others. We need to love ourselves before we can ever know how to love another. If we ourselves don't know what love is then how can we possibly tell another that we love them when we have not experienced love for ourselves.

Today most of this love that is floating around in the world is love that is based on lust. This sort of love does not carry respect, as real love can only ever come from the heart. Love has to be felt before it can be given to another. How can we give to another something we do not have? We can only give out something that belongs to us or is ours to start off with (love and respect). If we have not discovered that real feelings come from the heart then how can we hold someone's hand and tell them that we love them.

I say the word 'belong' as we all know that nothing in this world actually belongs to us but love can belong to us as it's linked to our hearts that belongs to our soul. That true and pure love that comes from our pure hearts is linked to our soul and that sort of love can never be turned into lust. We were made to care and share not to take and take. Most people have no respect for themselves or for the other person involved in their relationship. As soon as they set their eyes on someone all they will think about is love that is based on lust. That lust love is not eternal and will not last for very long as lust belongs to our senses of desire.

In reality one person is meant to be with one person at a time. Even in the Bible and our spiritual readings it clearly states to commit adultery is a sin and it is very wrong to lead people on by telling one lie after another just because we have turned our beautiful bodies into a lustful minded body as though we were an animal. Once again, if our conscience played an important part in our lives we would never even dream of having an affair with another or to use anyone just because we want a lustful pleasure that will only last for a short period of time.

If we are true and honest with ourselves then we need to be asking ourselves quite honestly that if we already have a partner then what can the other person give us that is going to be so different to what we can share with our own partner? How can we be unfaithful to our loved ones? That is one thing throughout my life that I have not been able to understand as to why people have affairs with others when deep inside of their hearts they must know how wrong it is?

Again it all comes back to controlling our senses. If we can learn to control our monkey minds then we should be able to control our senses as they are only worldly desires that last only for a very short period of time. We need to make a start somewhere to start to take control over ourself and desires. We have become slaves to our senses and our desires. These worldly desires will start to lock us up and keep us as their prisoners (weakness overtakes). Each time we have done something that deep in our hearts we knew it was wrong we always say the same thing.

'I knew it was wrong but I still did it'

Yes, we did it because we have now become the prisoners of our worldly desires and senses. We may be so very strong in our heads and with our tongues but the fact and truth is that we have now become very weak when it comes to our worldly desires and senses. When we have been having an affair with someone we know we shouldn't have been or have been stealing things that belong to another or are taking drugs and consuming too much alcohol; we act so brave and tough, shouting our mouths off and having no control over our tongues to what may come out of our mouths when we are found out or confronted.

No matter how wrong we are we show that 'I couldn't care less' attitude and may not be frightened or scared of anything or anyone because of our pride and ego. If we put our hands on our hearts and be honest with ourselves, do we not hear that faint frightened voice inside of us that tells us that it was wrong to have committed whatever it was that we may have done? That little frightened voice is our conscience that our senses and desires have kept locked inside of our temple bodies as a prisoner.

We can release ourselves and our conscience from being a prisoner to becoming the master of our bodies and of ourselves for ourselves and our consciousness. Yes, we are the Atma our conscience which is our soul. Every day we pick up the newspaper we read about so much that is happening all around us, the natural disasters are now beyond our control but we can still do our little bit by having respect towards Mother Earth. We can do this by changing ourselves and in the way we think, behave and act. So, let's stop polluting the whole world.

Let's have consideration for ourselves, our loved ones, our neighbours, and friends, for this beautiful world Mother Earth that we have been so graciously blessed with. The sun, sea, earth, stars, plants, trees, air, and sky; look how much Mother Earth has provided us with. Yet, we have learnt nothing about respecting the environment that we are living in. Instead we are so busy focusing on taking things that don't even belong to us, chasing money and wanting more of it and using that money on affairs, drugs, alcohol and gambling.

All this is leading us further and further away from our true identity and spiritual paths that we were all put on this earth to live for. To be a spiritual person one does not have to be religious. Religion and spirituality are two different things.

'Religion is a personal faith. We can all have it, but it's of our own choice'.

To be spiritual is a way of living of how we conduct ourselves in the way that we want to behave as a person, being honest and loyal towards ourselves, which is our body, soul and mind. Being spiritual towards ourselves can only make us even better to being a good, considerate, kind and truthful selfless and understanding person towards ourselves. If we cannot understand our real inner self then how can we begin to understand other people around us?

We go to school from a young age as we all feel we need an education as having an education comes almost compulsory, whilst spirituality is very similar. We can only become better people and souls by learning about our real inner souls, mind, thoughts, senses and feelings. Let it be education or spirituality we never stop learning because every day we are learning something new about the outside world that we are living in and about ourselves inside of our bodies or about our personalities.

We will never stop learning about ourselves until that last breath is taken and we are no more the body everyone recognises us as. Even then we were never our bodies as our soul was linked to our bodies but the soul is never attached to the body. This is because we have had many lives and many bodies. We need to take a few seconds or minutes to go within ourselves so that we can listen to our inner voice which is our Atma. That can only ever be done by remaining quiet and silent. That is called meditation or being in tune with our higher soul (Atma).

A lot of people mistake religion with spirituality, they say 'But I don't believe in religion and I don't want to be religious'. To be spiritual is so very different to being religious. We are focusing only on our mind, thoughts, attitude and Atma. Mainly on our inner body so that we can make changes in the way that we act and behave to be able to take more control over our senses that lead to our desires. By doing this we can change ourselves and our health can improve as most of our illnesses arise due to the way we think. We need to become more positive and let negativity slip out of our minds, thoughts and lives.

We do not need negativity as it causes us our downfalls all created by ourselves. Let's right now close our minds and put negativity in a balloon and watch it disappear up into the sky, 'out of sight out of mind'. Now, we need to focus on positivity, we need that in our lives as much as we need the air that we breathe. We know that without air we cannot survive, where without positivity in our lives we cannot survive either. Let's all hold hands and promise ourselves that from this moment for evermore we will always be very positive in our everyday lives.

No matter what happens or things may not turn out as we would like them to, we will always have a positive attitude towards everything, accept the good with the bad; accept the ups with the downs for life is full of ups and downs. We will have good and bad times, happy and sad times, we will have laughter and tears. Always remember that our downfalls will always prepare us for when we are up. All this will help us to develop in our everyday living as we are learning something new every day. Every day is so very different from yesterday and from tomorrow.

It's like the song, 'Yesterday is dead and gone, and tomorrow is out of sight'.

We can only ever live in the present; never can we live in the past or the future. Can we do anything about what may have happened in the past? No, we can only learn from it and move on. We can live in either our past which stops us from moving on into our future. If we keep looking into our past then how can we move forward as we cannot be in two places at one time? Time waits for nobody, so whilst our heads are turned to our past looking and watching our past events we are standing still in one place as the time is till ticking and moving on.

Why are we either wasting precious time looking at something that we cannot change nor do anything about? We can move on and never make those same mistakes again (they were not mistakes, only errors that we can do differently next time). We are only fools if we make the same mistake twice as first time was a learning point for us and as I have already said our mistakes are our errors. They should only happen once for us to learn from and then to move on to the next error as life is all about learning.

Let's talk about the things that we may have done out of character. Whether we have been taking drugs, had to steal, cheat, lie or have become an alcoholic, had a number of affairs or have done different things that we wouldn't normally do as a person. Why do we have affairs? Many people do this because they begin to feel that their partner no longer understands them or are not fulfilling their requirements and needs. They see someone and due to the circumstances day by day they begin to develop the urge of wanting something whatever the different reasons, it is either out of reach or within their league. Therefore the situation becomes more of a challenge, the more that we can't have it the more we want it.

There are situations where seeing other married couples having affairs have influenced them and they then have had the affairs. Seeing someone else meeting up in secret dangerous places where they don't wish to be seen together in secret has somehow made it very exciting for them both and it now has become a challenge that they may still wish to pursue.

The affair may last for a short period of time or a long time but in the end someone always ends up getting hurt. Whether it is the children or one of the partners, but someone will always end up getting hurt. I have yet to see a happy ending where affairs are concerned. Lies begin pouring into those kinds of relationships.

Taking Drugs

More times than not it is the people who have got more money than sense, they begin to earn so much money, first comes the clothes and the jewellery then the big homes and holiday homes along with a row of prestige cars then comes along the drugs. We may be at a party or at a gathering where plenty of alcohol is available, whilst being sober we may turn around and say no, but once that alcohol intoxicates our minds we may have no idea of what is happening around us or to us. We have one drink we feel we are in control, we have a few more drinks and then a few more and then there is no stopping us to alcohol or to drugs, we think it is only money but do we stop to think what harm and danger those drugs may be bringing into our lives. We can lose everything and all our loved ones. Do we know what we are capable of doing whilst under the influence of alcohol or drugs? We can do anything when we do not have control over our senses. Or there are the other people who are taking these substances but do not have the money but they begin to cheat, steal, deceit and lie, they can take anything that does not belong to them just to fulfil their desires even if it means taking a child's savings. How long does that desire last? A few hours, and what do we do? All that we are doing is telling more lies, stealing and then we want stronger substances until one day we never wake up again.

The only people who lose out will be our loved ones, who have had no choice but to see us slowly killing and destroying ourselves. This is because we didn't need anyone's help as we felt we were always in control. 'We need to help ourselves, before others can help us'. If we wanted to help ourselves then we had a choice and we could have asked for help, to stop at any time as there is so much help available.

111

I have yet to meet anyone who intoxicates his/ her senses and is still able to be in control. The only thing that was in control was the drugs or the alcohol or even the foolish people who have sold these substances. All they are concerned about is making money, and couldn't care less about the pocket, health or your loved ones feelings. All they want is your money, and lots more of it. Or else, why would they be involved with such things in the first place? If only these people had a conscience they would know what is right and what is wrong.

There is nothing wrong in wanting to earn a good amount of money so that we can better our ways of living but, there is a right way of earning money through sheer hard work, with honesty and dignity. If we ever earn money by taking short cuts, that money will always be 'easy come, easy go'. Money like that will never last and yet if we earn even five pounds through sweat and hard work watch that five pounds outstretch its value.

Yes, it is up to each individual how they choose to spend their money as they have earned it, please think very careful about how we spend our money.

'Waste is haste'. In Indian we call money 'Lakshmi' (mother goddess of money). To waste food, time and money is not good for us or for our spiritual growth.

I am sure there are others in this world that feel they don't need money, name and fame as these three things are not going to buy health, happiness or time. What can money buy, that they don't already have? Most of the people on this earth today are chasing after money, name and fame. Yes, we all need money in the way that we are living to survive but only enough to put food in our stomachs and for every day bills and maybe a little bit put away for a rainy day. Just a little from that save it for the less fortunate.

The real happiness and contentment is within ourselves, it lies within each and every one of us. Our journey in life is to find our real inner self which is like being on a treasure hunt. We have all been given a map and a key which lies within ourselves, but only we are able to go within ourselves, reach within for that key and unlock our hearts. Once, we have been able to do that we will see the real priceless gems of our personalities that lie within each and every one of us. To achieve this we don't have to go to great lengths, cause inconvenience, and cause ourselves any financial loss as it can be done in the simplest of ways.

We also don't have to be dependent on any one else as we are capable of doing this all by ourselves, through meditation which is linking us with our higher souls. Meditation is something that can be done throughout the day even whilst carrying on with our everyday chores.

Our ego, jealousy, pride and resentment have buried that treasure so deep inside of us that we can no longer feel or see it. That is the most important treasure any amount of money or worldly goods could ever take its place. If we are lucky and fortunate enough to be able to go within our deep inner self and start to look for that treasure, happiness and contentment we would never feel the need to search for anything else ever again. These two things, happiness and contentment, are the most important tools we will ever need to thoroughly be equipped with in order to survive.

Once we have been able to find our lost inner self we will not be in need of anything else as there is nothing inside of us or on this outer world that can replace or come anywhere near our happiness and contentment. We can be living in a castle, have a dozen prestige cars, lots of servants but unless we can find that happiness and contentment within how can worldly things give us ever-lasting happiness?

Chapter Eleven

I wish to dedicate this to all the special souls that have come and gone from my life. I wish to thank each and every one of you as you are the ones who have taught me different lessons through the experiences. There may be some things that I may have liked and others I have disliked. There have been some of you who have made me smile and laugh and for those precious moments I will be forever grateful. There have been good and bad times. Through my learning process I realised the errors and mistakes that I had once made, however even for those mistakes I am grateful as those situations I was compelled to face are the ones that taught me the most about myself and the world. From them I learnt to face my fears and still with determination, courage and faith walk forward and continue the purpose I was destined to do. At the end of the day we are all on a soul journey.

I pray to the Great Divine Universe that let me fill the hearts and lives of others with great joy and happiness. If kind words do not come out of others mouth then please teach those to speak no words as words once spoken cannot ever be taken back. I also pray to the Great Universe to give me the strength to be able to help others selflessly and unconditionally. Guide me to love unconditionally and to become even more humble and always keep my feet firmly on the ground so that I never forget who I am and what my purpose in life is.

Always keep me reminded on the saying 'Never look down at anyone on your way up, as you may meet them on your way down'. So for the many people that came into my life to teach me of all the different things I'm thankful even for the ones I may have not entirely understood or agreed with but it again taught me that life isn't always a bed of roses. We have to be able to accept the good with the bad. Everything that has happened to me in life has taught me so much. They were all lessons for me that I needed to learn, to help me to develop everything about myself. The biggest lesson to learn is to forgive each and every one and to hold no resentment against anyone or anything. For I have no enemies, the real enemy was myself to myself. Remember whatever you see in other people is always a reflection of yourself looking back at you like holding up a mirror.

'Forget the good you have done for others and the harm others have caused you'- Baba

The other thing I learnt was patience. It is necessary to be patient within yourselves before you can go any further. In order to be able to reach out to others you need to first reach within. So, once again a big heartfelt thank you for making me realise who I really am and not the person I thought I was, or the person you all thought I was.

From where I first started this journey even I struggled and it will come of no surprise if even with some concepts in this book you find you struggle with. However due to the kind souls still here, coming in disguises as my family, friends, neighbours and associates were in fact tremendous contributors to the discovery of my real inner self.

Throughout my life I have given and taken, I have forgiven and forgot all the souls who have borrowed from me and never given back but also helped me to learn to give selflessly and unconditionally. I have realised that all these things money and wealth was never really mine in the first or the last place. For I own nothing in this world. I do not really exist at all; this is a dream for me. As soon as I wake I will see the reality of this dream for myself. I know that I will wake up and say, 'thank God it was only a dream' although it felt very much real. We are all on a stage, playing different roles and soon as the play is over and the last curtain falls, we will all get off the stage and go our separate ways. We all come alone into this world and will leave all alone. So, who belongs to whom?

This life for me is like a passing cloud, nothing in this world is real as its all temporary. Why have I spent so much time chasing after this and that when nothing was really mine? Nothing or no one was ever mine. I used to think that money was this and that whilst money comes and goes, morality comes and grows. I was so lucky to have had so many good people that took so much of their time and effort just to teach me lessons. Whatever those lessons were good or bad, happy and sad certainly educated me. After all, the end of education is character. We can study and have a degree but the real education is how we conduct ourselves in our everyday living for that is the end of education. I want to say a big thank you to each and every one for taking out the time and making the effort to read this special message that I am sharing with you. With all my heart I want to say that I love each and every one of you as we are all one. The words that I have written are from the language of love and have come from the bottom of my heart, I pray that with my words I have not hurt anyone's feelings as that is not my intention at all. Some may say how can I say that I love you all when I do not know you all, but I can say that we are living and sharing the same earth and breathing in the same air, we came into this world the same way and will depart the same way so how does anything separate us from one another for we are all brothers and sisters from one big family called love and light. So may you all succeed on your individual soul journeys and I wish you the very best of luck, love, light and harmony always.

Sarb